P
O
L
L
Y
O
N

The Spirit of Homosexuality

Romel Duane Moore Sr.

Prayer Changes Things (PCT) Publishing
7551 Kingsport Road
Indianapolis, Indiana 46256

Scripture quotations are from the King James Version of the Bible, unless otherwise noted.

Cover design by Michael Covin.

Printed in the United States of America.

Edited by Margaret Rose Mejia.

ISBN: 9781793955142

The name satan is intentionally not capitalized.

TABLE OF CONTENTS

INTRODUCTION

While growing up in the inner city of Chicago in the 70's and 80's and going to high school in Michigan, I remember seeing very few people who were homosexuals and virtually none who were transgender. Occasionally, there was one male in most families, in our community, who was thought to have feminine ways and depending on the population of the high school, maybe one or two effeminate males in our Michigan high schools. Unlike the norms of the Millennials today, the presence of homosexuality was simply taboo. Like most things in life, what humans do not understand, we usually fear and judge out of ignorance. In 2002, I started a church in Fort Wayne, Indiana. To my great surprise, at least fifty percent of the congregation were either "gay" or had immediate family members who were "gay." They came to the church, regularly. Out of my fear and lack of knowledge, (since I grew up in a generation where homosexuality was virtually unheard of), I would find a way to insert the Divine judgement of Sodom and Gomorrah whenever I knew a homosexual was sitting in Service. It wasn't because I wanted every "gay" person to think they were going to hell. It was because I had never seen so many homosexuals from where I was from and it seemed they were coming to the church I was pastoring to make a point to me. I was going to let them know, that I was definitely not having it at the church I pastored. One night, the Lord impressed upon my heart that many of the "gays" in the community were coming to my church because they knew I would give them the truth. I believe the Lord was directing me to stop beating them up and love them. I obeyed God and set aside my seemingly homophobic attitude. I began treating them as I would anyone under God's care. Anyone who says they do not have stereotypical ways and mindsets are fooling themselves. It takes God many years to truly cleanse us from the hatred, racism, and ignorance we learned as we grew up. I learned that the homosexual community who attended my church loved God with all their hearts and many of their stories were horrific. They already knew their lifestyle was not in line with God's Word and they truly desired to do His will. There is no seminary or Bible college that can really prepare a person for real life ministry. It is "on the job training" and only those who have God's heart will lead the people without doing too much harm because of our own personal issues and biases. I welcomed many "gays" who came to church deep in the grip of homosexuality and they were able to change their lives and do their best to live according to the Bible, by the grace and power of God. They were talented, faithful, and the kind of person every pastor prays for concerning commitment and loyalty. The problem is never God or His Word. It is always His representatives who are still under construction. There is much the homosexual community has to offer the Body of Christ and it is the Christian's assignment to properly reach them through God's grace and love and lead them to eternal life. It does not matter if you believe a person is born homosexual or not because we all must be Born Again.

1

ORIGINS

And Noah awoke from his wine, and knew what his younger son had done unto him.

Genesis 9:24

The Bible does not detail the origin of homosexuality. However, I believe God left us enough breadcrumbs to figure it out. What is infamously known as the curse of Ham is really the curse of Canaan. Noah would not have cursed Canaan for Ham's offense. Therefore, it is logical to conclude that the sin was committed by Canaan. After Noah's deliverance from the Great Flood, Genesis 9:18 says this:

And the sons of Noah, that went forth of the ark, were Shem, and Ham, and Japheth: and Ham is the father of Canaan.

It is not a coincidence that Ham is mentioned as the father of Canaan when nothing noteworthy is going on at the time. Ham had more than one son and Canaan was not Ham's eldest son. The Scripture is setting the stage for an important event that is about to take place and mentioning Canaan as the son of Ham is a breadcrumb for us to follow and connect in the next scene that reveals the story of Noah's drunkenness and nakedness. Genesis 9:22-25 says:

And Ham, the father of Canaan, saw the nakedness of his father, and told his two brethren without.

And Shem and Japheth took a garment, and laid it upon both their shoulders, and went backward, and covered the nakedness of their father; and their faces were backward, and they saw not their father's nakedness.

And Noah awoke from his wine, and knew what his younger son had done unto him.

And he said, Cursed be Canaan; a servant of servants shall he be unto his brethren.

The Old Testament is written in Hebrew and there isn't a Hebrew word for *grandson*. The Scripture states that when Noah awoke from his wine he knew what his younger son did to him. We assume his younger son is Ham since Ham was the one who told his other brothers about his father's nakedness. However, it could refer to his grandson Canaan, as the younger son. Since the moment the natural eyes of Adam and Eve were opened and they knew they were naked, they were ashamed. Since the fall of man, seeing someone naked has been a part of the curse. Adam and Eve immediately covered themselves with fig leaves to cover their nakedness. It was against Old Testament Law (*Leviticus 18:6-18*) to see any relative naked, including in-laws. This law insinuates that nakedness is connected to sexual relations. Noah cursed his grandson Canaan after Canaan saw Noah's nakedness because Noah believed that his grandson had sexually assaulted him. It states that Noah knew what his younger son did to him. This definitely insinuates that something more than seeing him naked occurred. Noah was the only righteous man of his generation before the Flood and I do not think he would curse his grandson for the sin of his father Ham. I do not believe Noah would curse all the descendants of his grandson, unless it was for an "unforgiveable act." This is why I believe Canaan sodomized Noah after finding him drunk on wine.

Scripture records the open lifestyle of homosexuality in Genesis chapter 19 in the cities of Sodom and Gomorrah. Ironically, the first time Sodom is mentioned is in the lineage of Canaan. Genesis 10:19 says:

And the border of the Canaanites was from Sidon, as thou comest to Gerar, unto Gaza; as thou goest, unto Sodom, and Gomorrah, and Admah, and Zeboim, even unto Lasha.

Noah, his wife, their three sons, and their wives survived the Great Flood. They were responsible for repopulating the earth. The last thing they wanted to witness was some of the same sins that caused the Flood, in the first place. This may have been the motivation behind such a harsh retribution for what happened to Noah. Noah spent over one hundred years building the Ark. He didn't build it to exclude people from the Ark, but it was built to save lives. Whatever Canaan did to Noah must have warranted Divine judgement to the point that God was going to honor what Noah declared. Noah lived six hundred years before the Flood among the most wicked people who provoked God to send the Flood in order to destroy all flesh. In all the centuries that Noah lived in before the Flood, the Scripture doesn't record Noah being violated sexually. It had to be especially disturbing to Noah when it happened to him after the Great Flood and by his very own grandson.

BEFORE THE FLOOD

Genesis chapter six records the alien invasion of angels from Heaven who took their choice of women on earth to marry. Their forbidden union produced the hybrid race of giants. This detestable race of half angels and half humans single-handedly assisted in the proliferation of evil on earth before Noah's Flood. Genesis 6:4-5 says:

There were giants in the earth in those days; and also after that, when the sons of God came in unto the daughters of men, and they bare children to them, the same became mighty men which were of old, men of renown.

And God saw that the wickedness of man was great in the earth, and that every imagination of the thoughts of his heart was only evil continually.

Immediately after mentioning the presence of giants in the earth, the next Scripture informs us that God saw the wickedness of man and how every imagination of the thoughts of man's heart was only evil continually. This was not by happenstance. These fallen angels taught their evil giant offspring how to manipulate and pervert universal laws. The fallen angels also taught them witchcraft, wizardry, sorcery, magic, and the dark arts. These giants possessed supreme intelligence. They were a hybrid race and their angelic fathers taught them how to continue the perversion of crossbreeding with the rest of creation. The fallen angels taught these perverted acts to mankind and this increased evil on Earth. They began to successfully crossbreed nature like vegetation, insects, animals, and eventually man with animals. This is where the legend of vampires and werewolves originated. 2Samuel 23:20 speaks of *"lionlike men of Moab."* The purpose of this alien invasion was to stop the prophesied seed of the woman from coming to full fruition.

After the fall of man in the Garden of Eden, God prophesied that the seed of the woman would have enmity with the seed of the serpent and the seed of the woman would crush the serpent's head. Therefore, the enemy wanted to infiltrate a forbidden wicked hybrid race of giants to greatly assist in the contamination of mankind's genetics. We do not know to what extent the sinister breed of giants infiltrated the race of men, but it can be concluded it did infiltrate mankind (genetically) and their practices to the point where every imagination of the thoughts of man's heart was evil continually. Consequently, God had to destroy all living things in order to save the race of man.

Homosexuality was a part of these forbidden sexual practices because it directly affected the seed of man and man's ability to reproduce its own kind. The enemy's plan was to crossbreed the race of man and change his DNA, eliminating the ability of man to procreate through same sex relationships. Homosexuality was propagated and the only use for the female gender was for reproducing the homosexual genetic code. This plan worked so well that the enemy attempted to use the same strategy after the Flood. Genesis 6:4 says that there were giants in the earth in those days and after that, as well. This is how different races of giants are referenced in Scripture after the Flood. Many people read Old Testament passages where God commands the extermination of entire races of people by the nation of Israel. A little more research will unveil how those groups of people were connected to the wicked race of giants. Their diabolical DNA had to be completely destroyed. Whether it was Divine judgement against a certain tribe who procreated with a giant race or Divine judgement against a region like Sodom and Gomorrah, (havens for the homosexual lifestyle), the theme is clearly the protection of mankind's genes from alien and unnatural contamination and degeneration.

2

BLACK OUT

From the very beginning, homosexuality has profound roots in the black community. In order to understand this from biblical history, we must review the genealogy of nations from Noah's three sons after the flood. It is biologically impossible for two Caucasian people to reproduce black offspring. However, it is biologically possible for two black people to have white offspring. Noah's second eldest son, Ham, was a black man. This means both Noah and his wife were black or at least one of them was black. Ham's name means *black, hot, and swarthy.*[1] Ham's bloodline is recorded in Genesis 10: 6-13:

And the sons of Ham; Cush, and Mizraim, and Phut, and Canaan.

And the sons of Cush; Seba, and Havilah, and Sabtah, and Raamah, and Sabtechah: and the sons of Raamah; Sheba, and Dedan.

And Cush begat Nimrod: and he began to be a mighty one in the earth.

He was a mighty hunter before the Lord: wherefore it is said, Even as Nimrod the mighty hunter before the Lord.

And the beginning of his kingdom was Babel, and Erech, and Accad, and Calneh, in the land of Shinar.

Out of that land went forth Asshur, and builded Ninevah, and the city of Rehoboth, and Calah,

And Resen between Ninevah and Calah: the same is a great city.

And Mizraim begat Ludim, and Anamin, and Lehabim, and Naphtuhim,

Noah's eldest son, Shem became the father of the Mongoloid people populating the areas of the Middle East, Asia, and Asia Minor. Noah's second son, Ham, is the father of the Negroid people who inhabited the continent of Africa. Noah's third son, Japheth, is the father of the Caucasoid people, populating Europe and parts of Asia called Eurasia. Nimrod was the first world leader after the Great Flood. He was Ham's grandson. Some Bible scholars believe Nimrod was a giant because the wording used to describe him was similar to the description of the giants before the Flood. Genesis 6:4 says:

There were giants in the earth in those days; and also after that, when the sons of God came in unto the daughters of men, and they bare children to them, the same became mighty men which were of old, men of renown.

The description of Nimrod recorded in Genesis 10:8-9 states, *"And Cush begat Nimrod: he began to be a mighty one in the earth. He was a mighty hunter before the Lord..."* *Mighty one* is the Hebrew word *Gibbor* meaning, *powerful, warrior, tyrant, champion, chief, giant, mighty one, and strong man.*[2] It comes from a root word meaning, *to be strong, and act insolently.*[3] Giants before the Flood were called *mighty men* and this is the same Hebrew word *gibbor* that describes Nimrod as a *mighty one.* This means the fallen angelic race infiltrated the human race once again through the bloodline of Ham. Other giant races could be found throughout the Old Testament and usually within the bloodline of Ham. Giants were scattered throughout the Promised Land and this territory was also known as Canaan Land. Canaan was the fourth son of Ham.

Nimrod was the mastermind behind the building of the Tower of Babel and the leader of the building of the first cities of Babylon: Erech, Accad, Calneh and Ninevah. The earth had one language at this time. However, God had to confuse their language. This is where we get the story behind the word *babel*. The tribes under each of the sons of Noah retreated to their own territories because of this confusion of languages. Genesis 10:5 says:

By these were the isles of the Gentiles divided in their lands; every one after his tongue, after their families, in their nations.

After God confused mankind's language, it caused them to scatter and the tribes settled in their families and nations. God divided the land mass of the earth into continents. Genesis 10:25 informs us:

And unto Eber were born two sons: the name of one was Peleg; for in his days was the earth divided; and his brother's name was Joktan.

Peleg means *earthquake, separation through grace, cleaving, cutting in two, dividing, and separating.*[4] He was named Peleg because the people of earth experienced the continental divide during the time of his birth. This was by design, after man's language was confused and the tribes were scattered. Each divided continent had its own tribal people and language that differed from the rest of the world. Africa and Asia Minor were inhabited by Ham's sons. Let's look at the meaning of the names of Ham's four sons. Ham's firstborn son's name is Cush. His name is translated *Ethiopia* and means *firelike, burned, blackened, and combustible.*[5] His tribes inhabited the land of Ethiopia. Ham's second son's name is Mizraim. His name is translated *Egypt* and his tribes populated the area of Egypt. Phut was Ham's third son. The Libyans of Africa are the descendants of Phut.[6] The fourth son named Canaan established the Canaanite tribes who inhabited the land God promised to Abraham and his seed. This includes the territory of Jerusalem.

SODOM AND GOMORRAH

We've already established that Sodom and Gomorrah was part of Canaan's territory. Canaan and his tribes were predominantly black people according to Genesis chapter ten's list of nations. Let's look at the reasons the Scripture states that God judged the cities of Sodom and Gomorrah and the cities of the plains.

God visited Abraham to inform him concerning the Divine judgment that He was about to unleash on Sodom and Gomorrah because Abraham's nephew, Lot and his family lived there. He stated in Genesis 18:20, "Because the cry of Sodom and Gomorrah is great, and because their sin is very grievous." After God allowed Abraham to negotiate with Him, God agreed that if He could find ten righteous people in the city, He would not destroy it. However, there wasn't even ten righteous found in the city. Therefore, God sent two angels to deliver Lot and his family before destruction came. When the angels entered Lot's house, this is what occurred as recorded in Genesis 19:1-11:

And there came two angels to Sodom at even; and Lot sat in the gate of Sodom: and Lot seeing them rose up to meet them; and he bowed himself with his face toward the ground;

And he said, Behold now, my lords, turn in, I pray you, into your servant's house, and tarry all night, and wash your feet, and ye shall rise up early, and go on your ways. And they said, Nay; but we will abide in the street all night.

And he pressed upon them greatly; and they turned in unto him, and entered into his house; and he made them a feast, and did bake unleavened bread, and they did eat.

But before they lay down, the men of the city, even the men of Sodom, compassed the house round, both old and young, all the people from every quarter.

And they called unto Lot, and said unto him, Where are the men which came in to thee this night? bring them out unto us, that we may know them.

And Lot went out at the door unto them, and shut the door after him,

And said, I pray you, brethren, do not so wickedly.

Behold now, I have two daughters which have not known man; let me, I pray you, bring them out unto you, and do ye to them as is good in your eyes: only unto these men do nothing; for therefore came they under the shadow of my roof.

And they said, Stand back. And they said again, This one fellow came in to sojourn, and he will needs be a judge: now will we deal worse with thee, than with them. And they pressed sore upon the man, even Lot, and came near to break the door.

But the men put forth their hand, and pulled Lot into the house to them, and shut to the door.

And they smote the men that were at the door of the house with blindness, both small and great: so that they wearied themselves to find the door.

The men of Sodom weren't just homosexuals, they were lawless. I am acquainted with many homosexual men and I couldn't imagine them behaving like the men of Sodom. Paul gives us a detailed list of the reasons God judged Sodom and

Gomorrah. Their sexual preference was only one reason for their judgement.

For this cause God gave them up unto vile affections: for even their women did change the natural use into that which is against nature:

And likewise also the men, leaving the natural use of the woman, burned in their lust one toward another; men with men working that which is unseemly, and receiving in themselves that recompence of their error which was meet.

And even as they did not like to retain God in their knowledge, God gave them over to a reprobate mind, to do those things which are not convenient;

Being filled with all unrighteousness, fornication, wickedness, covetousness, maliciousness, full of envy, murder, debate, deceit, malignity; whisperers,

Backbiters, haters of God, despiteful, proud, boasters, inventors of evil things, disobedient unto parents,

Without understanding, covenantbreakers, without natural affection, implacable, unmerciful:

Who knowing the judgment of God, that they which commit such things are worthy of death, not only do the same, but have pleasure in them that do them.

Romans 1:26-32

As listed above, lusting for the same sex was only one of the sins. Jehovah is a merciful, gracious, and loving God. The Scripture is clear: He wills that none should perish, but all would come to repentance. He is not an unforgiving Judge Who exists just to punish His creation. He is not walking around with a pen and pad recording every little wrong thing we do so He can justify punishing us. God so loved the world that He gave His only Begotten Son. First, there is grace. Then, there is judgment. God gives us all time and space to hear His Voice, and respond to His loving prods toward our hearts to ask forgiveness for our sins, and come into covenant with Him. God is not intimidated by our sins. Jesus paid the price for every human sin possible, including murder, hatred, pedophilia, rape, incest, and wrath. There is a small minority of people who hate God and arrogantly defy His Will. After time and space are given to them to repent, Paul informs us that God will turn them over to a reprobate mind.[7] Jesus said He did not come to judge the world, but to save it.

The men of Sodom wanted to rape the two angels whom God sent to save Lot's family and any others who wanted to side with righteousness. It reminds me of what Jesus went through as He came to save the Jews. The Jews were the ones who demanded that He be crucified. The same evil men who surrounded Lot's house in attempt to rape the angels, could have escaped the imminent judgment. Lot offered his two daughters to the men who surrounded his house. However, they refused the women because they only wanted to gang rape men. The most tragic and insulting part of the story is that Lot's daughters were married, but still virgins. This means Lot's sons-in-law were "gay." The men of Sodom basically told Lot they did not want any "chickens." They said, "Where's the beef?"

The only reason Lot was not violated by the men of Sodom was because Lot's uncle, Abraham, was the one who delivered them from the four *Tidal Kings* after they were defeated and captured.[8] Upon their return to their cities, Lot must have been promoted to a position such as Mayor, because when the angels entered the city of Sodom, Lot was sitting in the gate. Only high-ranking members of the city sat in the gates of the cities in those days. The four *Tidal Kings'* army was not to be trifled with because they defeated Sodom and Gomorrah, the cities of the plain and also some tribes who had giant races. However, the Kings of Sodom and Gomorrah witnessed Abraham defeat the four *Tidal Kings'* great army with just three hundred and eighteen of his personally trained men. Even though the men of Sodom were reprobates, they knew not to touch Abraham's family because he could do to them what he did to the four *Tidal Kings.* In essence, they owed their freedom to Abraham. This was the grace of God in action to the people of Sodom and Gomorrah as God allowed them to be freed when Abraham delivered Lot.

Sodom means *burning, consuming with fire; conflagration, secret intrigues, hidden wiles, covered conspiracies, place of bitumen or lime.*[11] *Gomorrah* means *overbearing, material force, tyranny, and oppression.*[12] The fires of lust and sin that burned in the hearts of the leaders and people of Sodom and Gomorrah would fall upon them to their demise. Their fire, secret intrigues, hidden wiles and covered conspiracies explains why they were overbearing, materially forceful, tyrants, and oppressors. Non-biblical sources record how Sodom and Gomorrah had beds in their streets that were used to rape anyone who passed by or ventured into their wicked cities.

The night before Divine judgement hit Sodom, the men spent the entire night attempting to get into Lot's house in order to do the unthinkable to the two visitors. This put a capstone on the judgment to come. The sad commentary concerning this story doesn't end with Sodom's destruction by fire and brimstone, but the fact that Lot's wife disobeyed the angels' instructions. The angels told them not to even look back when they fled the city. Lot's wife looked back and was turned into a pillar of salt.

Then after righteous Lot and his two virgin daughters successfully escaped and fled into the mountains, the daughters took turns getting their father drunk and committed incest by having sex with him in their desperate, perverted attempt to continue Lot's bloodline. Its no coincidence that Noah's drunkenness ended in incest and Lot's drunkenness did also. The Bible speaks clearly against drunkenness. *Ephesians 5:18*

Actor Anthony Rapp accused fellow actor Kevin Spacey (currently best known for playing U.S. Representative Frank Underwood in the Netflix fictional, political drama called *House of Cards*) of making sexual advances on him when Rapp was only 14 years old. Spacey who was 26 at the time, apologized on Twitter for "deeply inappropriate drunken behavior." As of November 16, 2017, there were fifteen men (teenagers through 30 years old), who came forward and accused Spacey of sexual harassment, assault, or attempted rape. Most instances involved alcohol. Also on November 16, 2017, 20 people came forward and reported inappropriate behavior by Spacey when he was working as artistic director at the Old Vic Theatre. Since then, "fresh accusations" have surfaced daily.

Both daughters were impregnated and gave birth to two males named Benammi and Moab. These two males became the fathers of the Ammonites and Moabites who turned out to be some of the worst sinners in Old Testament history. Moab became infamous for sacrificing their newborn babies to a demonic false god named Molech. It is no coincidence that the same year abortion was legalized in America, the American Psychiatric Association dropped homosexuality from the DSM as a mental disorder.

JUDAH

Abraham is a descendent of Noah's eldest son, Shem. Abraham had Isaac, and Isaac had Jacob. Jacob's name was changed to Israel and he had twelve sons who became the twelve Tribes of Israel. Israel's fourth son's name was Judah and from Judah's line would come the Kings of Israel and ultimately, Jesus Christ our Lord. However, early in Judah's life, something profound occurred that pertains to the subject matter. Genesis 38: 1-10 says:

And it came to pass at that time, that Judah went down from his brethren, and turned in to a certain Adullamite, whose name was Hirah.

And Judah saw there a daughter of a certain Canaanite, whose name was Shuah; and he took her, and went in unto her.

And she conceived, and bare a son; and he called his name Er.

And she conceived again, and bare a son; and she called his name Onan.

And she yet again conceived, and bare a son; and called his name Shelah: and he was at Chezib, when she bare him.

And Judah took a wife for Er his firstborn, whose name was Tamar.

And Er, Judah's firstborn, was wicked in the sight of the Lord; and the Lord slew him.

And Judah said unto Onan, Go in unto thy brother's wife, and marry her, and raise up seed to thy brother.

And Onan knew that the seed should not be his; and it came to pass, when he went in unto his brother's wife, that he spilled it on the ground, lest that he should give seed to his brother.

And the thing which he did displeased the Lord: wherefore he slew him also.

When Judah became a young man, he ventured off on his own for a season and became good friends with an

Adullamite man name Hirah. Judah married a Canaanite woman and had three sons by her named: Er, Onan, and Shelah. Remember it was Noah's grandson, Canaan, who sodomized Noah and that act resulted in Canaan's lineage being cursed by Noah. The homosexual cities of Sodom and Gomorrah were within the Canaanite borders listed in Genesis chapter ten. Now we find Judah marrying a Canaanite woman and God killed his two eldest sons. This is a rare occurrence in Scripture and deserves our attention. It states that Judah's firstborn son, Er, was wicked in the sight of the Lord and God slew him. Judah's second son, Onan, was instructed to do what was an Eastern custom. The next brother was to marry the deceased brother's wife in order to continue his bloodline. However, Onan wanted to the enjoy the pleasure of being intimate with his brother's wife, but refused to do what was necessary to carry on his brother's name, and spilled his seed on the ground. God slew him for this offense. You might ask, *"What in the world did Er and Onan do that warranted a Holy God to immediately end their lives?"* The execution of Onan gives us the clue needed. This story was all about continuing the bloodline of Judah. The blessing is always appointed to the firstborn son and Judah's firstborn, Er, was wicked in the sight God. I believe Er was participating in homosexual acts and God did not want the bloodline of the Tribe of Judah that Jesus would proceed from to be connected to these homosexual acts. Judah chose to marry a Canaanite woman and Er's homosexual behavior was probably a generational curse within the Caananite woman's tribe. God was not going to allow it in the Tribal Line of Judah.

As aforementioned, Divine judgement usually followed behavior that contaminated human DNA. Sin was a product of man's fall, but the crossbreeding of angels' DNA with humans' DNA, and the infiltration of homosexuality in the bloodline clearly brings about the wrath of God. Since Judah's bloodline was predestined to bring in the Christ, the beginning of His line was important. Judah's second son was also judged because he refused to continue the lifeline of the tribe. This is not a pretty story and many sins are committed by Judah and those involved. However, God's purpose is clear in preserving the bloodline of Judah for the coming Messiah.

PRAISE AND WORSHIP

Homosexuality reared its head at the very beginning of Judah's lineage. *Judah* means *praise* and the number one position where homosexuality can be found in the black church today is on the praise and worship team. It is never a surprise to see a homosexual choir director or praise and worship leader in the black church. This has always been the one area homosexuality was accepted in the African American Church. It is no coincidence that the "Godfather of Gospel Music," Reverend Dr. James Edward Cleveland was "gay." God did not accept it in Judah's bloodline and it should not be accepted in praise (Judah) today. The person who leads us in worship is only second to the worship. When the church is "gifted and talented" oriented rather than "godly character and anointed" oriented, there will always be an open door for perversion.

We cannot ignore the fact that the territory of Sodom and Gomorrah belonged to Canaan, Noah's grandson who sodomized Noah and was cursed by him. The black community in America has experienced history repeating itself as we see a great proliferation in this generation of men participating in the homosexual lifestyle. Over fifty percent of the men in American prisons are black. However, black men only make up fifteen percent of the total population. Sixty-five percent of black families suffer from the absence of their fathers. The rise of "gay" black men add to the great deterioration of the black family structure. The good news is that just like God gave an opportunity to the inhabitants of Sodom and Gomorrah to repent, God desires to save homosexuals' lives instead of destroying them. He is Giver of life and takes no pleasure in the destruction of man. The Bible says that hell was created for satan and his angels, not for man. Anytime mankind enters the torture of hell, it breaks God's heart. The Scripture says in Hebrews 3:15, *"To day if ye will hear his voice, harden not your hearts..."* Every day we have the blessing and opportunity to change our course of life and turn from our sins. God takes no pleasure in the destruction of the ungodly. Today is the *"Day of Salvation."* No matter how strong of a pull you feel like the homosexual lifestyle has on you, it is not greater than God's love for you and the Blood of Jesus Christ. There is nothing about our lives He cannot heal, fix, and deliver. Call on the Name of Jesus!

3

SONS OF BELIAL

The nineteenth chapter of the Book of Judges records one of the most debased, sadistic stories in all of Scripture. A man from the Tribe of Levi travels to his father-in-law's home to get his concubine who left home to fool around. After the father-in-law's repeated requests to get his son-in-law to stay, the man from the Tribe of Levi finally leaves with his concubine and male servant to head home. The journey home led them through the territory of the Tribe of Benjamin. As they traveled, it got late and a *good Samaritan* (a man) offered to house them for the night. After entering the *good Samaritan's* home, some men of the city called *sons of belial*, a demonic faction of the Tribe of Benjamin. *Sons of belial* was any person who was considered wicked, worthless, lawless, or licentious. *Sons of belial* surrounded the house and demanded the man to give them the Levite so they could sexually abuse him. The man begged this horde of perverted sadists not to do such a thing and offered his daughter and the Levite's concubine to have for their own twisted pleasure. However, the *sons of belial* demanded to have the Levite but the Levite gave his concubine to the band of deviants. This is what the Scripture says:

And the man, the master of the house, went out unto them, and said unto them, Nay, my brethren, nay, I pray you, do not so wickedly; seeing that this man is come into mine house, do not this folly.

Behold, here is my daughter a maiden, and his concubine; them I will bring out now, and humble ye them, and do with them what seemeth good unto you: but unto this man do not so vile a thing.

But the men would not hearken to him: so the man took his concubine, and brought her forth unto them; and they knew her, and abused her all the night until the morning: and when the day began to spring, they let her go.

Then came the woman in the dawning of the day, and fell down at the door of the man's house where her lord was, till it was light.
Judges 19:23-26

Before I deal with the homosexual aspect of this story, I must speak about the *elephant in the room* in this horrific story: society's disregard and the total lack of value of women, in those days. Since the fall of humanity in the Garden of Eden, up until today, in most parts of the world, women have been treated like property and used for the sexual pleasure of men. Thank God for the *Me Too Movement* in America today, exposing the abuse of women and fighting for their equal rights and respect. I didn't want to include this story, in this book, because reading Judges chapter nineteen in the Bible again, disturbed me to my core. Writing about it is ten times more difficult. However, I am a messenger of truth and this story is in the Scriptures for a reason. Therefore, I need to talk about it.

This story sounds very similar to that of Lot and the homosexual men of Sodom. In both stories, men of the city heard about strangers entering their city, and came and surrounded the house where the strangers entered. In both stories, the evil, perverted men of the city demanded that the strangers (men) be released to them for wicked and debased abuse. Also, in both stories, women were offered as worthless "play things" in exchange for the men that the homosexuals sinisterly desired to sexually abuse. This story took a darker turn, as the Levite's concubine was actually released to the mob that consisted of hundreds of men. They sexually and physically abused her all night long. No reason is given as to why the master of the house did not follow through on his offer to give the *sons of belial* his daughter in addition to the Levite's concubine. And why wasn't the Levite's male servant offered to the men? We cannot get past the fact that these Benjamites did not want the females, but showed up violently demanding the males. They were deviant, practiced homosexuality, and were willing to use violence, if necessary, to get what they wanted. They moved in unison as a mob and had no problem sharing one man between hundreds of men. I can't imagine anything more gruesome.

The rest of the tribes of Israel joined together to bring justice for the unforgiveable act of sexually abusing and murdering the Levite's concubine. The other tribes of Israel unified and approached the leaders of the tribe of Benjamin demanding the lives of the perverted men who murdered the concubine. However, the Tribe of Benjamin refused to adhere to justice. This caused Israel to attack them militarily. There were great losses in this war and ultimately the entire Tribe of Benjamin was brought to the brink of extinction. All of their women, children, and cattle were destroyed. Only six hundred men of Benjamin were left. As a result, Israel felt remorse for almost causing the total annihilation of one of their tribes. In the end, Israel went to a neighboring tribe and took four hundred virgins and gave them to the remaining six hundred men of the Tribe of Benjamin to marry and continue their lineage.

Let's look at the similarities of this story and that of the destruction of Sodom and Gomorrah again. Smoke like a furnace ascended from the judgment of Sodom. Judges 20:40 says:

But when the flame began to arise up out of the city with a pillar of smoke, the Benjamites looked behind them, and, behold, the flame of the city ascended up to heaven.

As aforementioned, the reason why the Old Testament has stories of God ordering the genocide of certain tribes and people groups is for one of two reasons: either their bloodline was connected to the mixing of human and angelic DNA or homosexuality had taken over their society. After the Tribe of Benjamin revealed itself as a homosexual tribe, Israel not only destroyed the men, but they also destroyed the women, children, and cattle. Why? I believe it is because the Israelites did not want the homosexual spirit to successfully propagate and contaminate the human gene pool. Israel executed Divine judgement on the Tribe of Benjamin, just as God demanded of other homosexual societies and tribes in whom fallen angels infiltrated and mixed angelic DNA with human DNA. God knew that their sole purpose was to hinder the prophesied Seed of the woman, Who is Jesus Christ, from coming to save man.

SODOMITES

Sodomite is defined as "An inhabitant of Sodom, a person who engages or practices sodomy." Webster dictionary defines *sodomy* as "A sexual crime against nature." The Bible does not call same sex sin "homosexuality" or "gay," but the name the

Scriptures give is *sodomy*. Here are some Scriptures about the sin of sodomy.

1 Kings 14:24 says:

And there were also sodomites in the land: and they did according to all the abominations of the nations which the Lord cast out before the children of Israel.

1 Kings 15:12 says:

And he took away the sodomites out of the land, and removed all the idols that his fathers had made.

Leviticus 20:13 states:

If a man also lie with mankind, as he lieth with a woman, both of them have committed an abomination: they shall surely be put to death; their blood shall be upon them.

Ezekiel 16:49-50 says:

Behold, this was the iniquity of thy sister Sodom, pride, fulness of bread, and abundance of idleness was

in her and in her daughters, neither did she strengthen the hand of the poor and needy.
them away as I saw good.

Jude 7 reveals:

Even as Sodom and Gomorrah, and the cities about them in like manner, giving themselves over to fornication, and going after strange flesh, are set forth for an example, suffering the vengeance of eternal fire.

1 Corinthians 6:9 says:

Know ye not that the unrighteous shall not inherit the kingdom of God? Be not deceived: neither fornicators, nor idolaters, nor adulterers, nor effeminate, nor abusers of themselves with mankind.

4

CIVIL RIGHTS

Revelation chapter nine gives us hidden wisdom concerning the spirit of homosexuality. Someone may ask the question, "Why are you referring to homosexuality as a spirit?" My answer is, "Because by nature, to be attracted to the same sex is unnatural." When man is tempted to participate in unnatural behavior it is because of demonic influence. Whatever is unnatural is a perversion of universal laws. It is natural for males to be attracted to females and it is sin for opposite sex couples to engage in intimacy before marriage. It is unnatural for males to be attracted to males and females to be attracted to females; and it is sin to engage in "gay" sex. The difference between the two scenarios is that one is natural and the other unnatural. Demonic activity is involved in much of what mankind participates in and the spirit of homosexuality isn't an exception to the rule. A demonic spirit of lust, sickness, or greed is no different than the demonic spirit of homosexuality. The only contrast is the temptation to be attracted to the same sex is unnatural. The same is true if an adult is sexually attracted to children. This is unnatural. If a human is sexually attracted to an animal, it isn't just sin, but it's unnatural. To be sexually attracted to the opposite sex is natural, but sin to participate in sex before marriage. To be sexually attracted to the same sex is unnatural and to participate in "gay" sex is sin.

CIVIL RIGHTS

Civil rights are defined as *the right of citizens to political and social freedom and equality.* African Americans fought for rights to be respected as humans. The Homosexual community want rights based on their choice of a sexual preference. It is not the same. All the "gay" community initially asked for was reciprocal beneficiaries (health insurance from their employers and other civil rights, like hospital visitations), and they got it. Then they demanded civil unions and they received it. They pushed for same sex "marriage" and they got it. The LGBT Community demanded "civil rights" until legally they received everything they asked for and they pretty much have everything they asked for, as of right now. So I ask the question, *"Why are so many in the 'gay' community still angry and not satisfied?"*

In Hawaii, the "gay" community approached the Church and the conservative family group called Hawaii Family Forum. They told them that if they passed the reciprocal beneficiary bill then they would not push for civil unions or same sex "marriage" in Hawaii. The majority of the Church and Hawaii Family Forum agreed and at the Senate Hearing the reciprocal beneficiary law was passed. In 2009, the "gay" community introduced the first civil unions bill (the infamous HB444) stating that if they (the Church in Hawaii and conservative groups) helped to pass civil unions the American Civil Liberties Union (ACLU) and pro-homosexual groups would not push for same sex "marriage." Civil unions became legal in Hawaii in 2013. Shortly afterwards, the ACLU and other homosexual advocates pushed for same sex "marriage." Each time, the homosexual advocates gave their word that if they got what they wanted they would not push for something else. However, each time they got what they wanted, the homosexual community went back on their word and did exactly what they stated they would not do.

The average "gay" person's standard of living is much higher than the average American in every category. I was doing accounting for Metro Railroad in Chicago, Illinois in the 90's when the homosexual community was still in its beginning stages of making headway. Housing and Urban Development (HUD) occupied one of the floors in our building and they had a transgender employee. I saw the man on a few occasions in the lobby and on the elevator. He was a Caucasian man in his mid-thirties. He had an unkempt beard and physically appeared pretty scruffy. However, he was dressed like a woman in an old-fashioned dress and heels. His legs were still very hairy and his appearance wasn't feminine. Metro Railroad sent a letter to all employees threatening immediate termination if an employee said or did anything remotely offensive, including looking at this one man disrespectfully. I could not believe the company was so violently afraid of this one man's supposed rights and were willing to discriminate against everyone else's rights. The HUD office soon moved out of the building and the subject never surfaced again. I was offended to my core concerning the letter because I never remembered anything remotely that aggressive being legislated by a company for the advancement of black people. However, I would never desire the rights of others to be violated in the ignorant attempt to defend my civil rights. The railroad company handled the situation in the most egregious manner and I lost all respect for the company. I could not wait to set myself up to be able to leave them.

No American homosexual has ever been denied the right to vote, eat at restaurants, use bathrooms, or attend schools, because of their sexual orientation. Therefore, how can the "gay" community demand civil rights when their civil rights were never violated. When statistics show the median "gay" person has a higher standard of living than the average person in the nation, one's argument cannot be civil rights. Civil rights were fought and won exclusively for African Americans. Homosexuals were not enslaved for 400 years. They were never the property of the racist whites in the South. They were never raped, abused, and sold like cattle. Their free labor for hundreds of years did not build the strength of the American economy. They were not stripped from their homeland and sold into slavery. They did not endure the most heinous living conditions on slave ships. They were not brought by force to a foreign land and sold like common animals. Their family structure was not destroyed and the men were not used as breeders to populate their master's workforce. Their women were not used as bed heifers for white male slave owners to molest, rape, and have sex with at their leisure. Homosexual family lineages were not destroyed and contaminated by hostile foreign seed that changed the identity and bloodline of their seed forever. The "gay" community hasn't had to live through Jim Crow racist laws, segregation, and hasn't been denied basic American rights. They have never been the last hired and the first fired. They are not followed like common thieves in the stores they enter and falsely accused of crimes on a daily basis. Dogs were never "sicked" on them during peaceful marches and water hoses were not violently sprayed on them just because they are "gay." Their greatest leaders were not assassinated. Have they experienced hatred, violence, and forms of discrimination? Definitely, and it should have never occurred. However, the powers that be and every American system has never been set up against the homosexual community. Ignorant individuals or small groups performed despicable acts against the "gay" community. African Americans had the spiritual, economical, educational, political, military, and criminal systems in America directly set up to oppose them with many still discriminating against blacks today. I ask, "What gives homosexuals the right to place themselves in the same category as African Americans demanding civil rights when their basic rights have always been respected and intact?"

Every new presidential administration has allowed other social and political movements to supersede the black agenda in America. On the same day President Trump was inaugurated, the Women's Rights Movement was in full protest and hijacked any chance of the Black Movement having any traction. Under President Obama's Administration, the homosexual agenda was in full swing. Since the Civil Rights Act of 1967 the black agenda has not had national attention and no real progress has been made. After the death of Dr. Martin Luther King Jr., many of the leaders of the Civil Rights Movement sold out and allowed the homosexual agenda to join their platform because they felt like that was the only way to at least be heard by "the powers that be." Every new presidential administration gave a seat at the table to every other social agenda, except the black agenda, since the Civil Rights Act. Under the first African American President, every study has shown how each category of black existence dramatically deteriorated and declined drastically. Unemployment went up, job opportunity declined, educational opportunities declined, welfare dependency rose, new businesses declined, family structure declined, etc. There would be no doubt about the fact that if America ever voted for a homosexual president, he or she would do everything in their political power to help advance the homosexual agenda. It's to be expected. George W. Bush was from Texas and an "oil man" and it was no surprise that he took care of Texas and the Oil Industry. For some reason, it was treasonous for African Americans to expect the first African American President to look out for the black community. Anytime I ask another black person, *"Why didn't Obama do anything for the black community?"* The mainstream media has done a great job in programming many to say, *"Well, Obama wasn't the president of Black Americans, but all Americans, and it wasn't his job to promote policies for just African Americans."* My rebuttal is, *"What people group did Deferred Action Childhood Arrivals (DACA) benefit?"* My answer is: Only illegal aliens. *"What people group did 'gay' marriage and transgender rights benefit?"* The answer is: Only "gays" and transgenders. *"What companies did the hundreds of billions of free government money benefit?"* My answer is: Environmental companies. *"What single terrorist nation did one hundred and fifty billion dollars with 15 billion in cash air lifted to them benefit?"* The answer is: Iran! *"What group of people did one trillion dollars of stimulus money benefit?"* My answer is: Crooked Bankers. So the first African American President, who was the President of all Americans and not just African Americans could help undocumented immigrants, "gay" and transgender people, failed environmental start-up companies, America's number one terrorist enemy, and greedy Wall Street Bankers, but he couldn't do a single thing to help his own people who disproportionately suffer in every known social category of America?" I say, "Hogwash!" Obama didn't do a single thing to help the carnage raging on in his home city of Chicago. Under Obama, Chicago had the highest crime rate in America, the highest taxes, and one of the states with the highest unemployment rate. I'm from Chicago and was as proud as anyone to witness the first African American President come from my city, but after the celebration and photoshoot was over, we expected results and got none!

SAME SEX "MARRIAGE"

If marriage was a human idea then humans would have the right and privilege to change its foundation and covenant as we saw fit. However, marriage was not a human idea. Marriage was a "God idea." And because it was God's idea, only God can change it and He has not saw fit to do so. God placed Adam in a deep sleep before taking a rib from him to make woman. God did not consult with Adam before making his wife, Eve. God didn't even inform Adam about what He was about to do. This was for a reason: so that man had nothing to do with the creation and covenant of marriage and will never have the power to change the marriage covenant. It does not matter if ninety-eight percent of all marriages end in divorce, it will forever be a covenant between a man and a woman because the One Who thought of marriage and created the first male and female to enter its covenant set it up that way. It doesn't matter if human government passes laws legalizing same sex "marriage" because until it's sanctioned by the One Who created the institution, same sex "marriage" will never be legal and blessed by the God Who created marriage. If God does not bless our unions, ultimately, they will not succeed.

For what shall it profit a man, if he shall gain the whole world, and lose his own soul? If God has the power to bless marriages, this means He also has the power to curse them. The Scripture teaches us, *"What therefore God hath joined together (in marriage), let not man put asunder."* Mark 10:19 Likewise, whom the Lord does not bring together, anyone can tear apart.

Under President Barack Obama, the homosexual community seemingly got everything they desired including same sex "marriage" and "gay" equality in the military. The man who sat under Pastor Wright in Chicago, Illinois for twenty years and ran for president confessing that he believed marriage was between one man and one woman, soon changed his stance on the subject and became homosexuals' greatest advocate. I could claim that maybe his true beliefs about the matter is connected to the book published about his homosexual affair entitled *Barack Obama & Larry Sinclair: Cocaine, Sex, Lies & Murder* but I will leave it to God. What we do know is that Obama was the first President of the United States to break from the long held tradition that marriage is between one man and one woman.

Government constitutions are separate and apart from God's Constitution, the written Word of God. As Christians, anytime our government laws do not line up and agree with God's Laws, according to Scripture, we are not bound to adhere to them. For instance, it is legal to sell, purchase, and use tobacco products that boldly state on its own packaging that smoking causes cancer and emphysema. Therefore, smoking is legal according to man's law but is directly contrary to God's Law that forbids us to do anything to harm our bodies because our bodies are "the temple of the Holy Ghost." In some parts of the world, it is legal to engage in sex with minors. If we lived in that part of the world, their laws would not agree with God's Laws and as Believers we would be required by God to abide by His laws. Matthew 10:28 makes this clear:

And fear not them which kill the body, but are not able to kill the soul: but rather fear him which is able to destroy both soul and body in hell.

The advancement of homosexual rights and their agenda in a society does not equate to approval by God. Proverbs 14:34 states, *"Righteousness exalteth a nation: but sin is a reproach to any people."* The moral compass of the people of a nation will ultimately determine how long that nation will exist in any reasonable degree of wealth and prosperity. Although public officials are elected by and for the people they represent, officials must always lead and govern from their own heart and sense of morality. If we know the will of the people we represent is evil and immoral, we must take a stand for what is right. We cannot stand for what unrighteous constituents demand. The elected official who stands for righteousness will stand justified before God, although he or she may be rejected by man.

5

SPIRIT OF HOMOSEXUALITY

I n the ninth chapter of Revelation, the spirit of homosexuality is revealed in prophetic detail. The images and symbolism given in the Book of Revelation unveils the true identity of this spirit and it is amazing. The chapter begins with this description:

And the fifth angel sounded, and I saw a star fall from heaven unto the earth: and to him was given the key to the bottomless pit.

And he opened the bottomless pit; and there arose a smoke out of the pit, as the smoke of a great furnace;

and the sun and the air were darkened by reason of the smoke of the pit.

Revelation 9:1-2

There is a striking similarity of what occurred when the angel opened the bottomless pit and what Abraham witnessed during the judgement of Sodom and Gomorrah. Genesis 19:27-28 says:

And Abraham gat up early in the morning to the place where he stood before the Lord:

And he looked toward Sodom and Gomorrah, and toward all the land of the plain, and beheld, and, lo, the smoke of the country went up as the smoke of a furnace.

Abraham saw smoke from the judgement of Sodom and Gomorrah in the form of fire and brimstone ascend like the smoke of a furnace. When the angel opened the bottomless pit there arose a smoke like a great furnace. The best way to interpret the Bible is to let Scripture interpret Scripture. This initial detail is "the bottomless pit was opened" and it gives us our first clue of who and what the passage is about to reveal. The second detail given is the beginning of the description of the spirit that ascended out of the bottomless pit.

And there came out of the smoke locusts upon the earth: and unto them was given power, as the scorpions of the earth have power.

Revelation 9:3

The spirits in the bottomless pit were not being released for the first time because they did not originate in the bottomless pit, but were bound there after the Flood. When the sins of a people, culture, and nation get to a certain level, it unlocks the gates of hell to propel the people to the next level of evil in order to render the justifiable judgment. Sin is like garbage. When we allow garbage to lay out openly long enough, it attracts rats. Human sin practiced lasciviously long enough attracts demons. Once the sin opens a foothold, in time, it will become a stronghold. Locusts in Scripture were used as agents of judgment. God used locusts as one of the plagues in Egypt. Locusts are used as agents of judgement in this passage as the fifth trumpet is blown to release another wave of judgment during the Great Tribulation. Joel 2:25 says:

And I will restore to you the years that the locust hath eaten, the cankerworm, and the caterpillar, and the palmerworm, my great army which I sent among you.

Each time the spirit of homosexuality is released in earth as judgment for perpetual sins of a people, they come on the scene like locusts and rapidly cover a region. In one generation, we've witnessed the great multiplication of homosexuality throughout the earth. It was given unto these demons (that looked like locusts) to have power, like scorpions of the earth have power. Revelation 9:4 states, *"And it was commanded them that they should not hurt the grass of the earth, neither any green thing, neither any tree; but only those men which have not the seal of God in their foreheads."* It is common for locusts to consume the greenery of the earth, like grass and leaves. However, these demonic spirits that are described as locusts were instructed not to harm any green thing on the earth, but to only harm the people who did not have the seal of God in their foreheads.

HORSES PREPARED FOR BATTLE

And the shapes of the locusts were like unto horses prepared unto battle . . .   Revelation 9:7

The shape of these demonic spirits were like "horses prepared for battle." The spirit of homosexuality began a movement and this movement is described as "horses prepared for battle." I cannot imagine locusts that are shaped like military horses. However, I definitely can understand the symbolism. The homosexual movement is exactly the personification of the imagery of "horses prepared for battle." From the time they began to publicly demand for equality, their movement was not passive. They did not simply sit back and wait their turn to be heard. The homosexual community stormed the halls of city, state, and federal government to demand what they desired. They galvanized their finances, voices, and political strength to change the legislative and judicial systems of America until they got everything they desired. They never had to fight for basic civil rights. However, from the very beginning they demanded civil unions, same sex "marriage," and even homosexual curriculum in the public school system.

When a small group of people gather united under a certain set of beliefs, it's called a cult. When that group and belief system grows into greater numbers, it's called a culture. Once you add yeast to flour, there is no way you can separate the two. Once a society allows homosexuality into its culture, it is impossible to get rid of it. The only way to remove homosexuality from any culture is for that society to fall. If you give the devil a foothold it will become a stronghold. Once homosexuality grows roots and becomes a part of the culture, you will see it in every facet of society. Less than thirty years ago, one virtually did not see homosexuality in any area of American society. However, today, major news anchors, talk show hosts, famous actors, actresses, musicians, designers, politicians, pastors, priests, singers and dancers are homosexuals. There isn't one American industry where homosexuality is not openly seen and represented. There is no way possible for their presence to be removed from American culture. Unless there is a great revival, a move of God in America and the homosexual community gives their hearts to Christ, in time, the only thing that can occur (without a revival), is judgement on the whole nation and a great fall. Any Bible scholar worth his or her weight will inform you that America is invisible in End

Time Prophecy, meaning that when the next great war occurs, America will either not be involved because of internal issues or it has already fallen from being the world power.

Rome was not defeated from external enemies, but it fell from internal corruption, deterioration, and sexual immorality with homosexuality at its core. The greatest government and military the world has ever known corroded from within as greed, godlessness, and sexual perversion destroyed its society. As Roman chariots assembled at the borders of every great nation on earth to conquer them, so has the homosexual movement assembled in America and the rest of the world in order to have their agenda legalized. This has not been a passive or uncontroversial movement. The homosexual movement was like "horses prepared for battle."

CROWNS LIKE GOLD

. . . and on their heads were as it were crowns like gold . . .   Revelation 9:7

Crowns are what kings wear and crowns in this passage signify the power and authority the homosexual possesses in everything he/she does. In Every industry they participate in, they are the leaders and creators. They wear the crowns in fashion, designing, singing, choreography, comedy, the culinary arts, theatre, acting, etc. They are literally the best at what they do. Their arrogance and boldness comes from this fact. Homosexuals know that no one can compete with them in their perspective arenas. In the entertainment industry, no one will do it better!

FACES OF MEN

. . . and their faces were as the faces of men. Revelation 9:7

The spirits of homosexuality have "faces of men." Men populated the spirit of homosexuality before the women propagated lesbianism.

HAIR OF WOMEN

And they had hair as the hair of women . . .
Revelation 9:8

What are the odds that the description of the spirit of homosexuality has "a face like a man" and "hair like women?" Even if I wanted to, I could not make this up. Whether or not you want to connect this to crossdressing or men wanting to look like women, the Book of Revelation hits it right on the head.

TEETH OF LIONS

. . . and their teeth were as the teeth of lions.
Revelation 9:8

Lions are the kings of the jungle and are superior predators. The description of "having teeth like lions" represents the boldness and tenacity whereby this spirit will speak and devour all who attempt to oppose, disagree, or stop them. Freedom of speech is heralded anytime the homosexual community speaks their rhetoric. However, all who disagree with their agenda are cursed, threatened, protested, and some have even physically hurt their opponents. These are hate crimes committed against heterosexuals by the homosexual community.

In Hawaii, a pregnant woman was on the side of the road on the windward side of the Island of Oahu holding a sign. The sign said to "Vote No to Same Sex 'Marriage." An advocate of same sex "marriage" hit her and her sign with his car and she was dragged about 20 feet with her sign. The woman suffered contusions, scratches, scrapes and her leg was injured. She went to the doctors to check on the baby. Thank God that she and her baby didn't suffer any major injuries. This is one example of a hate crime committed against a heterosexual woman by a homosexual male. She was merely practicing her right to Freedom of Speech but was stopped ferociously by a homosexual opponent.

The owner of Chick-fil-A participated in his right to Freedom of Speech when he stated that he believed marriage is supposed to be between one man and one woman. The homosexual community didn't honor his right to free speech and because his free speech did not agree with their agenda, they immediately revealed their "teeth like lions" as they cursed him and mobilized to protest inside his fast-food chain. This protest backfired on them as Christians came out by the hundreds of thousands to support Chick-fil-A and their sales went through the roof. The homosexual marches look nothing like the peaceful marches of black people during the Civil Rights Movement. The homosexual community use their "teeth like lions" to be loud, cantankerous, profane, and disrespectful. They curse God, Christ, the Church, and anyone or anything that disagrees with their agenda.

Chicago, Illinois is about to elect their first African American female as Mayor. Two African American ladies are the remaining candidates for Mayor and one is a lesbian. Her name is Lori Lightfoot and she is the underdog but has a very good chance of winning. I believe her sexual preference should not have anything to do with her ability to be an exceptional leader and no one should not vote for her if she is a better candidate. But Lightfoot has been accused of distributing thousands of flyers to citizens of the Chicagoland area stating.

We know we're going to win! All contracts, jobs, and employment newly assigned exclusively to gay people! With our people in City Hall, I promise to enforce the

Gay Equality Act. All churches will abide by the gay marriage laws. All public restrooms will be gender-free. All Public Schools will teach Gay History by mandate. School restrooms must be DE-SEGREGATED.

Anise Parker was elected as the first open lesbian Mayor of Houston, Texas. She sent out court ordered subpoenas demanding pastors hand over copies of any sermon that discussed her, homosexuality, and gender identity. She threatened their tax-exempt status if they spoke out against her sexual preference. The clergy's freedom of speech was ignored and Mayor Parker was ready to shut them down for speaking what they believed. This is two examples of this spirit having teeth like lions when it comes to furthering the homosexual agenda. Lions devour their prey and their teeth are the most dangerous part of them in a fight. The homosexual movement and their representatives have teeth like lions especially once they are in positions of authority. They will not apologize or have any remorse for anyone who gets in their way. There is no compromise or mercy. They will roar and completely devour anyone who opposes them.

BREASTPLATES OF IRON

And they had breastplates, as it were breastplates of iron . . .   Revelation 9:9

The breastplate is the part of military armor that protects the vital organs, mainly the heart, during battle. The spirit of homosexuality has a breastplate of iron. Iron is one of the strongest metals used in ancient times for war. This breastplate of iron represents the hardness of the hearts of those who have this spirit. A hard heart is the number one hindrance to man when God is tugging at our hearts to repent of our sins and turn from our evil ways. This imagery of "breastplates of iron" reveals to us the reprobate condition of many with this homosexual spirit. This also reveals the truth that their heart is impenetrable. Many who are seduced by this spirit are unrepentant because they are haters of God. God's grace is available for anyone who humbles himself and asks for it. However, God cannot and will not save anyone who rejects His great salvation. We are free moral agents and if we choose to die in our sins and go to hell, He will honor our choice. In battle, arrows can hit our breastplate. However, if our armor is strong enough, our breastplate will withstand the attack and will not harm us. The spirit of homosexuality has "breastplates of iron" and unfortunately, many times the armor surrounding their hearts rejects the darts of God's love and mercy that is sent to change their hearts and save them.

SOUND OF MANY CHARIOTS

. . . *and the sound of their wings was as the sound of chariots of many horses running to battle.* Revelation 9:9

The homosexual movement is signified as having the "sound of many chariots." This is connected with the description of "horses prepared for battle." In ancient wars, the army who possessed horses and chariots had the advantage over their enemy who only had foot soldiers. Horses can run over men and chariots are better than just having horses. This spirit is definitely prepared for war! Horses and chariots move faster than men on foot. The homosexual movement has not only moved swiftly within one generation, it also made a lot of noise as it progressed. The sound of horses and chariots in battle can be deafening. The homosexual movement was not a march like the Civil Rights Movement. It was a stampede, a military occupation with a battle cry, shouting aloud like a "sound of many chariots."

TAILS LIKE SCORPIONS

And they had tails like unto scorpions, and there were stings in their tails . . . Revelation 9:10

The Scripture records how the homosexual spirit was given power in the earth just like scorpions have power in the earth. This demonic spirit has "tails like scorpions." The main weapon the scorpion possesses is located in his tail. His tail holds a powerful stinger. It is no coincidence that the spirit of homosexuality has a "scorpion's tail." The deadly consequence of the homosexual lifestyle is found in his tail. The worldwide deadly diseases called Human Immunodeficiency Virus (HIV) and Acquired Immune Deficiency Syndrome (AIDS) come from anal sexual intercourse between two males. The stinger is in their tails. I can't make this up.

KING OVER THEM

And they had a king over them, which is the angel of the bottomless pit, whose name in the Hebrew tongue is Abaddon, but in the Greek tongue hath his name Apollyon.   Revelation 9:11

This demonic spirit has a king over them and his name in Hebrew is *Abaddon*. In Greek, this spirit is called *Apollyon*. *Apollyon* means *destroyer*. Imagine that. The leader of the spirit of homosexuality is a destroyer! This was revealed when homosexuality resurfaced on the scene in the 1980's along with the deadly disease called HIV and AIDS. Sodomy, better known as homosexuality is not just about same sex relations, but the enemy's ultimate goal and strategy is about destruction. The spirit of homosexuality has a king over it and his name means *Destroyer*! Destroyer of a life, family, society, and nations. But Romans 5:20 says, *". . . But where sin abounded, grace did much more abound."* Isaiah 53:5 says:

But He was wounded for our transgressions, He was bruised for our iniquities; The chastisement for our peace was upon Him, And by His stripes we are healed.

God so loved the world that He gave His only begotten Son, that whosoever believes in Him will not perish but have everlasting life. God takes no pleasure in the suffering of the wicked. It is His will that we all come to repentance and allow Him to heal and deliver us from every snare of the devil. Jesus loves the homosexual as much as He loves everyone else. Jesus died for the sins of the homosexual.

The Lord knows that eighty-five percent of homosexuals were molested and sexually abused as innocent children. This opened the demonic door to the spirit of homosexuality. He does not desire for the homosexual to continue living in the pain and agony of this reality. God wants to deliver him/her. God does not remove our past. However, He can heal us from it. Hebrews 4:15 AMP states, *"For we do not have a High Priest who is unable to sympathize and understand our weaknesses and temptations, but One who has been tempted [knowing exactly how it feels to be human] in every respect as we are, yet without [committing any] sin."*

The work of Calvary paid the price for every person bound by homosexuality and He is waiting to save, heal, and deliver any person from the homosexual lifestyle. The homosexual spirit must bow to the Name of Jesus! Apollyon is not greater or stronger than Jesus. Romans 10:13 says, "For whosoever shall call upon the name of the Lord shall be saved." Every person born into this world is in need of salvation and deliverance from sin. The homosexual, lesbian, and transgender is no different. Jesus died for the sins of the world, but we must recognize our sin and come clean

6

THE ANSWER

A close friend of mine experienced firsthand what it was like growing up with a "gay" sibling. From day one when her twin brother and sister were born, people noticed there was something different about her younger brother. At a very young age, instead of being interested in playing with trucks and things little boys like, he chose to prance through the house in his mother's high heels and play dress up. The young boy had two older brothers who beat on him because of his feminine ways and attempted to teach him how to play masculine sports. They ended up abusing him even more by knocking him on the ground and throwing the football at him for not being interested in or talented at male sports. The parents would stop the older brothers from roughing him up and the mother thought it was cute when he played dress up in her clothes. The father would simply tell him to take the clothes off.

By his teenage years, the twin brother spent as much time in the bathroom as his sisters. However, it was assumed that he was a very clean young man and took pride in his hygiene and appearance. He was always surrounded by girls in high school, had girlfriends, and went to the Prom with a girl. After his first year of college, the twin brother predominantly kept company with men. The family noticed he had hemorrhoids and always had to visit the physician relating butt issues. In college, the twins shared a computer at home. The twin sister went to her older sister and complained that each time she logged onto the computer male pornography and "gay" male dating sites were popping up. It was presumed that the computer had viruses, so she blew it off. Both of the twins were on a break during their college years and the twin sister walked in on her twin brother giving fellatio to another man. The twin sister was in shock and it damaged her for some time. She kept it secret for a while. One day, the sister twin called her older sister and told her what she caught her twin brother doing to another man. A few months later, the older sister called her brother and told him personally, that he did not have to hide who he was and they loved him regardless of his sexual orientation. He answered her stating, "Thank you."

The twin brother continued to hide his "gay" lifestyle until the season of getting married to his male companion drew near. Friends of the family assumed his fiancé was a woman and they really did not find out he was "gay" until the sisters informed the family that the man in many of the twin brother's photos was his soon-to-be husband. Others did not discover the truth until they saw the wedding photos. My friend informs me that presently he is very unhappy even though he has a doctorate and two masters degrees. He is also a successful entrepreneur and an excellent professional. The twin brother calls his older sister daily, complaining about his career and life. My friend says that ever since he came "out the closet," he has never found true happiness despite his upper class living. He is a perpetually miserable and disgruntled person. It doesn't matter who we are. Peace can only be obtained from the Prince of Peace.

Some years ago, I questioned God about the progress of the "gay" movement in America. "Why," I asked Him, "despite the prayers of the Saints, were they (homosexuals) seemingly getting the things they wanted from Congress?" The Lord impressed upon me how many in the "gay" community will not turn to Him until their supposed fight for rights came to fruition because as long as they felt like they had something to fight for, they would be blinded concerning the real truth of their lifestyle. The Lord impressed upon me how once they got everything they thought was wrongly withheld from them, then they would truly see the error of their ways and begin to turn to Him. Once all the external "enemies" are removed, the only enemy that would be left for them to deal with, individually, was the one in the mirror.

I preached at a church in Hawaii and at the end of the message I gave an altar call for salvation. The only person who responded was a man dressed like a woman. He used a female name and came to church that way. He seemed to be sincere when he repented of his sins and gave his heart to Christ. A few months later, I returned to the church to preach again and after the service I heard the church announcing the names of all those who joined the church and the church announced that same person as a man, using his original name. That was in 2016. As of today, he is still living as the male God created him to be. He loves the Lord and is in leadership in ministry, helping to win souls for Christ. When we know the truth and come to God admitting the error of our ways, He will save, heal, and deliver us. No matter who we are, if we ignore God's truth and determine to live in our sins, we will continue to suffer the consequences. The wages of sin is death but the gift of God is eternal life through Jesus Christ our Lord. None of us are exempt.

PERVERSION

If you listen to the individual stories of "gay" people, you will find that in most cases, they were molested or raped at some time in their youth. The perpetrators were either family members, close friends of the family, or a member of a religious community. Their stories are horrific and should have never happened. Does everyone who is molested or raped become or have homosexual tendencies? No. However, the majority of the men and women who participate in the "gay" lifestyle have been raped or molested. There is a demonic door opened in the life of every victim of rape and molestation because the act is perverted. The sexual appetites of people who have been raped and molested are forever changed.

The victims will either have a very aggressive and open sex life or they will regress and view sex as an undesirable and unclean act.

SAME SEX

If two people desire the same sex, why is it one of them always takes on the role of the opposite sex? If two men are attracted to each other, why does one of them have to be the female in the relationship? If two females are attracted to each other because they are not attracted to males, why is it (one hundred percent of the time) one of them takes on the role and function of a male, even to the point of looking like a man, acting like a man, and using artificial male sexual parts to perform sex? This is the ultimate contradiction. If you truly are not attracted to the opposite sex, you do not desire any of their functions or traits. If you are only attracted to men and masculinity, why is one always acting like a woman and performing feminine things? Why can't we ever find two totally feminine women and neither looking like or acting like the male? Why can't we find two totally masculine men looking like and acting like absolute masculinity? The reason why is because it is the contradiction that reveals the hypocrisy of same-sex relations. If same-sex relations are natural, why can't they reproduce? The answer is: because it's not natural. Without artificial insemination two females would not be able to give life. And without adoption or surrogates, two males would not be able to parent and father children. This confirms the truth: same sex relations were never supposed to exist.

LGBTQIA

LGBTQIA is an acronym for lesbian, gay, bisexual, transgender, queer or questioning, intersex and asexual.

Lesbian is *a homosexual woman.*

Gay is *(of a person) homosexual (used especially of a man).*

Bisexual is *sexually attracted not exclusively to people of one particular gender, attracted to both men and women.*

Transgender is *denoting or relating to a person whose sense of personal identity and gender does not correspond with their birth sex.*

Queer means *strange; odd.*

Intersexes are *people born with any of several variations in sex characteristics including chromosomes, gonads, sex hormones, or genitals.* According to the United Nations Office of the High Commissioner for Human Rights, intersex people *"do not fit the typical definitions for male or female bodies."*

Asexual is defined *without sexual feelings or associations.* Asexual individuals may still experience attraction but this attraction doesn't need to be realized in any sexual manner.

The initials in the official acronym for the homosexual categories seems to keep increasing. They have recently included the initial "Q" for *queer* or *questioning,* the initial "I" for *intersexual,* and the initial "A" for *asexual.* How can *questioning* be a sexual preference and a group of people deserving certain rights? It is beginning to look like a side show.

Now every confused and perverted microcosm of society is coming out of the woodworks. Recently, the New York Post printed an article on pedophiles claiming they have a genetic code that gives them a predisposition to desire and lust for children. They will be attempting to be recognized and demand the same rights the homosexual movement did. A good friend of mine showed this New York Post article to a homosexual co-worker and the co-worker was disgusted and said that the pedophiles' claims were ridiculous. My friend explained to him that was the exact way most Americans felt about the homosexual claims and asked him if he could see where all of this was going now that Pandora's box was open in our society? He had no comment. Now that America has allowed the door of perversion and sexual deviancy to be opened, it will have to deal with the deluge of every known deviant sexual behavior conceived out of man's evil, fallen heart. What will keep people who want sexual relationships with animals from demanding rights? What about rapists who want to pursue protection based on "quack science?"

When all the smoke clears, the only thing that will stand is God's Word. God's Word is truth and God had it correct from the very beginning. God made us male and female and He divinely designed us to be attracted to the opposite sex. And only through sexual relations with the opposite sex is life designed to come forth. If we have malfunctions with a Ford vehicle, we take it back to the Ford dealership because they are the manufacturer. Many of us have gotten used to taking things we purchase to unauthorized people to get our malfunctioned gadget fixed. We have taken this "stinking thinking" into our personal lives. The first people we call with most of our problems are the very people who do not have the wisdom or ability to fix our issues. Instead, we should bring our problems to God Who created us.

GENERATIONS

In the more liberal states, cities, and counties, homosexual-friendly curriculum has been implemented in American elementary schools. The most debased homosexual-friendly curriculum is in Hawaii. It's named *Pono Choices* and comes from a California curriculum. *Pono* means *righteousness*. However, there is nothing righteous about it. The curriculum was originally implemented without the knowledge or permission of the parents. A mother attended one of their meetings and found out it was in the schools and began to spread the word to other parents. Now, the school sends a letter home with the student asking the parent's permission if the student can be taught sex education. However, most parents don't know that this "sex education" is *Pono Choices*. *Pono Choices* redefines sex and biology. The curriculum calls the anus, a genital. Any moral parent would be outraged at the lewd diagrams the curriculum displays. This is where the future of American education is headed and we should be ashamed.

What we call normal, we cannot change. The difference between my generation and the Millennials, is the presence of homosexuality as normal. Outside of the truth of God's Word, there is very little keeping homosexuality from staying the new norm from this generation onward. As same-sex "marriages" increase and children are reared under their care, every following generation will become more accepting to this perversion. This makes the possibility of true reformation almost impossible. How can anyone believe children raised by same-sex parents are going to enter society as normal, sober-thinking adults? I am not including any statistics connected to the condition of children raised in same-sex households because every single study seemed to be tainted and biased on both sides. What I will say is that we cannot expect a blessing to come out of the curse. We cannot believe abnormality over normality. It's impossible to get light out of darkness. I feel deeply sorry for every innocent child who has to live in a same-sex environment. Do I believe same-sex parents love their children? Yes. Do I believe homosexual parents will rape or molest their children? No. I simply believe God created mankind, marriage, and family. Therefore, when we do not do things by His Divine design, we are foolish to expect wholeness, blessings, and eternal success from it. My personal opinion means nothing. I'm not smart enough to articulate intelligently concerning any of these issues. God's Word is my guiding Light. History has shown us that God got it right from the very beginning. Mankind's only safety is the Holy Bible. Bible stands for (Basic Instructions Before Leaving Earth).

One of the most important areas of our lives is our sexuality. Everyone who experiences confusion or a difference of opinion concerning their sexuality, should consult our Father God, first. Man is the product of six thousand years of sin and degeneration. The longer man remains in this downward spiral the more defects and perversion of God's original design and intent we will see surface. I personally do not know how to address every case of abnormality concerning others sexuality, but I know Who has all the answers and it is the One who made us. All things were made by Him and without Him was not anything made that was made. Would you take your broken-down Ford to Kellogg's Cereal Company to be fixed? Of course not. Why do we continue to take the broken areas of our lives to others who are clueless about putting us back together? God is not the Author of confusion. Proverbs 3:5-7 says:

Trust in the Lord with all thine heart; and lean not unto thine own understanding.

In all thy ways acknowledge him, and he shall direct thy paths.

Be not wise in thine own eyes: fear the Lord, and depart from evil.

I believe no matter how dark the issue is, God can put us back together again. He is the Potter and we are the clay. Many of us come to Him with the most broken situations imaginable. He cannot only heal us, He makes us whole. Jesus said He is the Vine and we are the branches and apart from Him we cannot do anything. *John 15:5*

THE ANSWER

One of the many areas the Church has been utterly failing at, is the issue of homosexuality. It takes no effort to issue damnation to anyone who does not believe and behave how we do. This was not the character of Jesus. He was accused by the religious elite of fellowshipping with the worst of society. Jesus told this same group of religious hypocrites, *"They that be whole need not a physician, but they that are sick."* *Matthew 9:12* I am not homophobic because I do not fear homosexuals. Why is it anyone who disagrees with homosexuals are considered homophobic? I love all people and my message to all people who do not know the Love of Christ is the same message Jesus preached; *Repent, for the kingdom of Heaven is at hand.* We were all born in sin and shaped in iniquity because of the fall of Adam. The answer is simple whether you are heterosexual, homosexual, lesbian, transgender, or bi-sexual and it does not matter if you believe you were born that way because in order to be saved we all must be Born Again and go through the precious blood of Jesus.

Prayer of Salvation

Heavenly Father, I come to you admitting that I am a sinner. I choose to turn away from sin, and I ask You to cleanse me of all unrighteousness. I believe your Son Jesus died so that I may be forgiven of my sins and made righteous through faith in Him. I call upon the Name of Jesus Christ to be my Savior and the Lord of my life. Jesus, I choose to follow You and I ask that You fill me with the power of the Holy Spirit. I declare I am a child of God. I am free from sin and full of the righteousness of God. I am saved. In Jesus' Name. **Amen**.

About the Author

Romel Duane Moore Sr. was born in Chicago, Illinois. He served as Pastor of Liberty Temple Full Gospel Church of Fort Wayne, Indiana for five years. Romel has worked in middle schools, group homes, and has served as director of a faith-based program called Unity of Love Family Reconnect, helping inmates readjust after being released from prison. He has worked closely with re-entry court programs, serving as a liaison between ex-offenders and re-entry court. Romel has taught in prisons and juvenile facilities in fifteen states. He has been a mentor with Big Brothers, Big Sisters and the Boys and Girls Clubs of America. Romel actively volunteers with American Red Cross. He holds crusades, feeds the homeless, and cares for the helpless. He is a twenty-year accounting professional and presently the Pastor of Kingdom Convoy in Honolulu, Hawaii. He has authored more than twenty books that's available on Amazon and Kindle. You may contact Pastor Moore for speaking engagements at (808) 397-4906.

Footnotes

[1] Definition of **Ham**. Ham's name means *burnt, swarthy, black, A son of Noah*, Genesis 5:32 7:13 9:18 10:1. Rand, W. W. Entry for 'Ham'. American Tract Society (ATS) Bible Dictionary Online; https://www.studylight.org/dictionaries/ats/h/ham.html. 1859. Accessed on 12/02/18.

Definition of **Ham** is *Cham* in the Hebrew #2526; the same as #2525; *hot* (from the tropical habitat); *Cham, a son of Noah*; also (as a patron.) *his descendant* or *their country*:- *Ham*. #2525 *cham* from #2552; *hot*:- *hot, warm*. #2552 *chamam*; a primitive root; *to be hot* (literally or figuratively):- *enflame self, get* (have) *heat, be* (wax) *hot*, (be, wax) *warm* (self, at). New Strong's Expanded Exhaustive Concordance of the Bible, Copyright © 2010 by Thomas Nelson Publishers. Published in Nashville, TN, by Thomas Nelson, Inc.

[2] Definition of **mighty one** is *gibbor* in the Hebrew #1368 meaning intents from the same as *#1397* (see Footnote #3) *powerful*, by implication *warrior, tyrant*:- *champion, chief*, x *excel, giant, man, mighty (man, one), strong (man), valiant man*. New Strong's Expanded Exhaustive Concordance of the Bible, Copyright © 2010 by Thomas Nelson Publishers. Published in Nashville, TN, by Thomas Nelson, Inc.

[3] Root word of **mighty one** is *geber* in the Hebrew #1397 from #1396; properly *a valiant man* or *warrior;* generally *a person simply*:- *every one, man*, x *mighty*. New Strong's Expanded Exhaustive Concordance of the Bible, Copyright © 2010 by Thomas Nelson Publishers. Published in Nashville, TN, by Thomas Nelson, Inc.

4 Definition of *Peleg* is *Peleg* in the Hebrew #6389 the same as #6388 and means *earthquake*; *Peleg, a son of Shem*:- *Peleg*. #6388 *peleg* from #6385; *a rill* (that is a small channel of water, as in irrigation):- *river, stream*. #6385 *palag* a primitive root; *to split* (literally or figuratively):- *divide*. New Strong's Expanded Exhaustive Concordance of the Bible, Copyright © 2010 by Thomas Nelson Publishers. Published in Nashville, TN, by Thomas Nelson, Inc.

5 Definition of *Cush* is *Kuwshiy* in the Hebrew #3569 means *patron* from #3568; *a Cushite*, or *descendant of Cush*:- *Cushi, Cushite, Ethiopian* (-s). #3568 *Kuwsh* probably of for. or.; *Cush* (or *Ethiopia*), *the name of a son of Ham*, and *of his territory*; also *of an Israelite*:- *Chush, Cush, Ethiopia*. New Strong's Expanded Exhaustive Concordance of the Bible, Copyright © 2010 by Thomas Nelson Publishers. Published in Nashville, TN, by Thomas Nelson, Inc.

6 Descendants of *Phut*. Phut also was the founder of Libya, and called the inhabitants Phutites, from himself: *The Works of Josephus* by Josephus, Flavius; Copyright © 1987 by Hendrickson Publishers, Inc.; Published in Peabody, MA. Excerpt found in *The Antiquities of the Jews*; Book 1: *From the Creation to the Death of Isaac*, Chapter 6: *How Every Nation Was Denominated From Their First Inhabitants*, Section 2 (130): The Children of Ham.

Definition of *Phut* is *Puwt* in the Hebrew #6316 of foreign origin; Put, a son of Ham, also the name of his descendants or their region, and of a Persian tribe:- Phut, Put. New Strong's Expanded Exhaustive Concordance of the Bible, Copyright © 2010 by Thomas Nelson Publishers. Published in Nashville, TN, by Thomas Nelson, Inc.

7 Definition of *reprobate*. This word is also used with reference to persons cast away or rejected because they have failed to

make use of opportunities offered them. M.G. Easton M.A., D.D., Illustrated Bible Dictionary, Third Edition, published by Thomas Nelson, 1897. https://www.biblestudytools.com/dictionary/reprobate/ Accessed on 12/23/18.

Definition of *reprobate* is *adokimos* in the Greek #96 means *failing to pass the test, unapproved, counterfeit.* New Strong's Expanded Exhaustive Concordance of the Bible, Copyright © 2010 by Thomas Nelson Publishers. Published in Nashville, TN, by Thomas Nelson, Inc.

[8] **The Four Tidal Kings** were
1) Chedorlaomer, King of Elam
2) Tidal, King of Nations
3) Amraphel, King of Shinar
4) Arioch, King of Ellasar
This can be found in Genesis 14:9.

[9] Blacks, Gays and the Church: A Complex Relationship by Corey Dade; 5/22/12; National Public Radio; https://www.npr.org/2012/05/22/153282066/blacks-gays-and-the-church-a-complex-relationship; Accessed on 12/24/18.

[10] https://www.usatoday.com/story/life/2017/11/07/kevin-spacey-scandal-complete-list-13-accusers/835739001/

[11] https://www.bbc.com/news/entertainment-arts-41884878

[12] LGBTQIA ?

Made in the USA
Columbia, SC
23 October 2024